My Gratitude Journal

7 Minutes Today
Leads to an Abundant
Life Tomorrow!

Linda McLean

*#1 International
Bestselling Author*

Quantity discounts are available on bulk orders.
Contact info@TAGPublishers.com for more information.

TAG Publishing, LLC
2030 S. Milam
Amarillo, TX 79109
www.TAGPublishers.com
Office (806) 373-0114
Fax (806) 373-4004
info@TAGPublishers.com

ISBN: 978-1-59930-408-3

First Edition

Dedication

This book is dedicated to all the those willing to take a chance on a daily basis to try something different to bring about positive change in their lives.

Acknowledgement

You might think that expressing gratitude in a gratitude journal would be an easy task. I personally find it to be the hardest part of writing a book! There are so many people in my life for which I am eternally grateful.

Here are a select few:

- Scot McLean, my supportive husband who, thankfully, is never truly surprised when I embark on a new quest.
- Brittany and Paige McLean, my amazing daughters who bring me joy consistently throughout our wonderful relationship.
- Brenda Do, who over a cup of coffee a few years ago helped me create the first version of the Gratitude Journal.
- Gina Hayden and Patti Knoles for creating the new journal face and layout.
- Louisa Tremann, my trusted friend and coworker, for her remarkable foresight in seeing what this journal should be and her exemplary editing to make it match that vision.
  Louisa, your dedication and commitment to deliver the best of the best is greatly appreciated.
- And of course, my best friend, Jesus, who without fail is always supporting me and directing me along my path in life.

Want more? Start with Gratitude.

If you want more – more happiness, better health, more wealth, more love, anything – then commit just 7 minutes a day to create it. This Gratitude Journal guides you through the simple, yet transformative process.

This is your personal "30-Day, Get Back on Track" program. Just start each morning and end each night with your journal. And you will surely experience positive changes in your life.

Gratitude Journal Instructions
Step 1:
Making a change requires effort and accountability. Find an accountability partner who will support you as you move through the journal for the next 30 days. Even better, gift your partner with a Gratitude Journal and hold each other accountable. Set a regular time each week for sharing changes you observed and discussing your progress.

Step 2:
Each morning, read the day's quote and ask yourself, "What is this saying to me today?" Jot your thoughts down. You may be tempted to skip this step – don't.

Step 3:
Fill in your day's grateful list. Quickly list 10 items you're grateful about. Don't over think it. Jot down whatever comes to mind. It can be as simple as the rich cup of coffee in your hand, a family member or a new job starting soon.

Thinking positive thoughts will create positive results. You'll see for yourself over the next 30 days. So if you start thinking "negative thoughts" during the day, think about or look at your gratitude list.

Take a deep breath. And move forward with a hopeful, believing heart that you're alright, life is wonderful and everything happens for a reason.

Step 4:

Set a goal. Change can only happen when you make a decision. Record a work/school goal you'd like to achieve by the end of the day. And record a personal goal you'd like to achieve by the end of the day.

Step 5:

Reflect and record. Before laying your head on the pillow that night, review your Gratitude Journal. Read your gratitude list. Reflect on your two goals, checking off what you achieved. Think about other accomplishments you made today. Write those items anywhere on the page too. Focus on what you're accomplishing – no matter how small you think it is. So long as you're moving forward, you're moving towards your goals. And that's huge.

Then picture the amazing day you will have tomorrow. The most powerful time to feed your subconscious is first thing in the morning and right before you go to sleep. When you drift off to sleep with peaceful, positive thoughts you sleep better, and your last thoughts sink deep into your subconscious. This subtly shifts your next day's actions in a way that helps achieve your goals and desires faster.

This Gratitude Journal is the powerful beginning of your new journey. During the next 30 days, you will unconsciously create your Roadmap to Success©.

Be sure to take a friend along for the ride, have fun and stay grateful.

All my best,

Linda

Daily Quote

*"You don't know where you are going
until you pick a destination."*

~ Linda McLean

What does this mean to me?

_____

_____

_____

_____

_____

_____

_____

_____

_____

_____

_____

_____

_____

Today, I am grateful For...

Date: ....

1. ....

2. ....

3. ....

4. ....

5. ....

6. ....

7. ....

8. ....

9. ....

10. ....

Goals for today:

Personal: ....

Work/School: ....

End of day wrap up:　　　　　　Yes!

Personal goal accomplished?　　☐

Work/School goal accomplished?　☐

Other accomplishments: ....

....

....

Daily Quote

*"Chart the course, commit to your plan,
be prepared to handle problems,
and expect the results you desire."*

~ Linda McLean

What does this mean to me?

_____

_____

_____

_____

_____

_____

_____

_____

_____

_____

_____

_____

_____

Today, I am grateful for...

Date: _____

1. _____

2. _____

3. _____

4. _____

5. _____

6. _____

7. _____

8. _____

9. _____

10. _____

Goals for today:

Personal: _____

Work/School: _____

End of day wrap up: *Yes!*

Personal goal accomplished?   ☐

Work/School goal accomplished?   ☐

Other accomplishments: _____

_____

_____

Daily Quote

"A positive attitude is not a destination. It is a way of life."

~ Linda McLean

What does this mean to me?

_____

_____

_____

_____

_____

_____

_____

_____

_____

_____

Today, I am grateful for...

Date: _____

1. _____

2. _____

3. _____

4. _____

5. _____

6. _____

7. _____

8. _____

9. _____

10. _____

Goals for today:

Personal: _____

Work/School: _____

End of day wrap up: Yes!

Personal goal accomplished?   ☐

Work/School goal accomplished?   ☐

Other accomplishments: _____

_____

_____

Daily Quote

"Plan purposefully,
prepare prayerfully,
proceed positively,
pursue persistently."

~ Linda McLean

What does this mean to me?

_____

_____

_____

_____

_____

_____

_____

_____

_____

_____

_____

Today, I am grateful for...

Date: ....

1. ....

2. ....

3. ....

4. ....

5. ....

6. ....

7. ....

8. ....

9. ....

10. ....

Goals for today:

Personal: ....

Work/School: ....

End of day wrap up: Yes!

Personal goal accomplished?   ☐

Work/School goal accomplished?   ☐

Other accomplishments: ....

....

....

Daily Quote

*"Choose friends and associates compatible
with your goals and interests."*

~ Linda McLean

What does this mean to me?

_____

_____

_____

_____

_____

_____

_____

_____

_____

_____

_____

_____

_____

_____

Today, I am grateful for...

Date: _____

1. _____

2. _____

3. _____

4. _____

5. _____

6. _____

7. _____

8. _____

9. _____

10. _____

Goals for today:

Personal: _____

Work/School: _____

End of day wrap up: Yes!

Personal goal accomplished?   ☐

Work/School goal accomplished?   ☐

Other accomplishments: _____

_____

_____

Daily Quote

"There is no danger of developing eyestrain from looking on the bright side of things. Where can you improve your viewpoint?"

~ Linda McLean

What does this mean to me?

_____

_____

_____

_____

_____

_____

_____

_____

_____

_____

Today, I am grateful for...

Date: _____

1. _____

2. _____

3. _____

4. _____

5. _____

6. _____

7. _____

8. _____

9. _____

10. _____

Goals for today:

Personal: _____

Work/School: _____

End of day wrap up: Yes!

Personal goal accomplished?   ☐

Work/School goal accomplished?   ☐

Other accomplishments: _____

_____

_____

Daily Quote

"Learn to spot opportunities and seize them courageously. What opportunities have you been presented with lately that are worthwhile?"

~ Linda McLean

What does this mean to me?

_____

_____

_____

_____

_____

_____

_____

_____

_____

_____

_____

_____

Today, I am grateful for...

Date: ....

1. ....

2. ....

3. ....

4. ....

5. ....

6. ....

7. ....

8. ....

9. ....

10. ....

Goals for today:

Personal: ....

Work/School: ....

End of day wrap up: *Yes!*

Personal goal accomplished?   ☐

Work/School goal accomplished?   ☐

Other accomplishments: ....

....

....

Daily Quote

*"Be willing to accept occasional small setbacks.
Consider it a lesson in disguise."*

~ Linda McLean

What does this mean to me?

_____

_____

_____

_____

_____

_____

_____

_____

_____

_____

_____

_____

_____

Today, I am grateful for...

Date: _____

1. _____

2. _____

3. _____

4. _____

5. _____

6. _____

7. _____

8. _____

9. _____

10. _____

Goals for today:

Personal: _____

Work/School: _____

End of day wrap up: Yes!

Personal goal accomplished?   ☐

Work/School goal accomplished?   ☐

Other accomplishments: _____

_____

_____

Daily Quote

"Enjoy today and expect an abundance."

~ Gina Hayden

What does this mean to me?

_____

_____

_____

_____

_____

_____

_____

_____

_____

_____

_____

Today, I am grateful for...

Date: _____

1. _____

2. _____

3. _____

4. _____

5. _____

6. _____

7. _____

8. _____

9. _____

10. _____

Goals for today:

Personal: _____

Work/School: _____

End of day wrap up: Yes!

Personal goal accomplished?   ☐

Work/School goal accomplished?   ☐

Other accomplishments: _____

_____

_____

Daily Quote

*"Give thanks for talent. Tap into your strength,
that is where you will find your talent. Use whatever
talent you have been given to the highest level you can
reach and embrace it with joy and a thankful heart."*

~ Linda McLean

What does this mean to me?

_____

_____

_____

_____

_____

_____

_____

_____

_____

_____

_____

_____

_____

Today, I am grateful for...

Date: ....

1. ....

2. ....

3. ....

4. ....

5. ....

6. ....

7. ....

8. ....

9. ....

10. ....

Goals for today:

Personal: ....

Work/School: ....

End of day wrap up: Yes!

Personal goal accomplished?   ☐

Work/School goal accomplished?   ☐

Other accomplishments: ....

....

....

Daily Quote

*"Laughter relaxes the body, boosts the immune system,
triggers the release of endorphins, and protects the heart.
Engage in laughter today."*

~ Linda McLean

What does this mean to me?

_____

_____

_____

_____

_____

_____

_____

_____

_____

_____

_____

_____

Today, I am grateful for...

Date: _____

1. _____

2. _____

3. _____

4. _____

5. _____

6. _____

7. _____

8. _____

9. _____

10. _____

Goals for today:

Personal: _____

Work/School: _____

End of day wrap up: Yes!

Personal goal accomplished?   ☐

Work/School goal accomplished?   ☐

Other accomplishments: _____

_____

_____

Daily Quote

"Health is a gift that you give yourself. One step at a time,
one day at a time leads you to a higher level of health.
A healthier you can give the gift of your talents to others.
Serve others by serving yourself first."

~ Linda McLean

What does this mean to me?

_____

_____

_____

_____

_____

_____

_____

_____

_____

_____

_____

Today, I am grateful for...

Date: _____

1. _____

2. _____

3. _____

4. _____

5. _____

6. _____

7. _____

8. _____

9. _____

10. _____

Goals for today:

Personal: _____

Work/School: _____

End of day wrap up: Yes!

Personal goal accomplished?   ☐

Work/School goal accomplished?   ☐

Other accomplishments: _____

_____

_____

Daily Quote

*"Remember that we first make our habits,
and then our habits make us. What habit(s) would
you like to develop or what habit(s) would
you like to eliminate?"*

~ Linda McLean

What does this mean to me?

_____

_____

_____

_____

_____

_____

_____

_____

_____

_____

Today, I am grateful for...

Date: ....

1. ....

2. ....

3. ....

4. ....

5. ....

6. ....

7. ....

8. ....

9. ....

10. ....

Goals for today:

Personal: ....

Work/School: ....

End of day wrap up: *Yes!*

Personal goal accomplished?   ☐

Work/School goal accomplished?   ☐

Other accomplishments: ....

....

....

Daily Quote

*"Devote some time to community support.
Giving to others fills your personal gas tank."*

~ Linda McLean

What does this mean to me?

_____

_____

_____

_____

_____

_____

_____

_____

_____

_____

_____

_____

_____

_____

Today, I am grateful for...

Date: _____

1. _____

2. _____

3. _____

4. _____

5. _____

6. _____

7. _____

8. _____

9. _____

10. _____

Goals for today:

Personal: _____

Work/School: _____

End of day wrap up: Yes!

Personal goal accomplished?   ☐

Work/School goal accomplished?   ☐

Other accomplishments: _____

_____

_____

Daily Quote

"Do not wait for an opportunity to be all that you want it to be. Step up, move, and keep moving in the direction of your goals."

~ Linda McLean

What does this mean to me?

_____

_____

_____

_____

_____

_____

_____

_____

_____

_____

_____

_____

Today, I am grateful for...

Date: _____

1. _____

2. _____

3. _____

4. _____

5. _____

6. _____

7. _____

8. _____

9. _____

10. _____

Goals for today:

Personal: _____

Work/School: _____

End of day wrap up: Yes!

Personal goal accomplished?   ☐

Work/School goal accomplished?   ☐

Other accomplishments: _____

_____

_____

Daily Quote

"Celebration is a joyful occasion to mark a special event and is magnified when shared with others. Take time to think of what and how you can celebrate."

~ Linda McLean

What does this mean to me?

_____

_____

_____

_____

_____

_____

_____

_____

_____

_____

_____

_____

Today, I am grateful for...

Date: ....

1. ....

2. ....

3. ....

4. ....

5. ....

6. ....

7. ....

8. ....

9. ....

10. ....

Goals for today:

Personal: ....

Work/School: ....

End of day wrap up: *Yes!*

Personal goal accomplished?   ☐

Work/School goal accomplished?   ☐

Other accomplishments: ....

....

....

Daily Quote

*"Your purpose explains what you are doing with your life.
Your vision explains how you are living your purpose.
Your goals enable you to realize your vision."*

~ Bob Proctor

What does this mean to me?

_____

_____

_____

_____

_____

_____

_____

_____

_____

_____

_____

_____

_____

Today, I am grateful for...

Date: _____

1. _____

2. _____

3. _____

4. _____

5. _____

6. _____

7. _____

8. _____

9. _____

10. _____

Goals for today:

Personal: _____

Work/School: _____

End of day wrap up: Yes!

Personal goal accomplished?   ☐

Work/School goal accomplished?   ☐

Other accomplishments: _____

_____

_____

Daily Quote

*"A true optimist sees new opportunities
for accomplishment with each new day."*

~ Linda McLean

What does this mean to me?

_____

_____

_____

_____

_____

_____

_____

_____

_____

_____

_____

_____

_____

_____

Today, I am grateful for...

Date: _____

1. _____

2. _____

3. _____

4. _____

5. _____

6. _____

7. _____

8. _____

9. _____

10. _____

Goals for today:

Personal: _____

Work/School: _____

End of day wrap up: Yes!

Personal goal accomplished?   ☐

Work/School goal accomplished? ☐

Other accomplishments: _____

_____

_____

Daily Quote

"You are the captain of your own vessel.
Aim for a port and use your heart as a guide."

~ Linda McLean

what does this mean to me?

Today, I am grateful for...

Date: ....

1. ....

2. ....

3. ....

4. ....

5. ....

6. ....

7. ....

8. ....

9. ....

10. ....

Goals for today:

Personal: ....

Work/School: ....

End of day wrap up: Yes!

Personal goal accomplished?   ☐

Work/School goal accomplished?   ☐

Other accomplishments: ....

....

....

Daily Quote

*"Inspiring others to follow by example
is the hallmark of a wise leader."*

~ Linda McLean

What does this mean to me?

_____

_____

_____

_____

_____

_____

_____

_____

_____

_____

_____

_____

_____

Today, I am grateful for...

Date: _____

1. _____

2. _____

3. _____

4. _____

5. _____

6. _____

7. _____

8. _____

9. _____

10. _____

Goals for today:

Personal: _____

Work/School: _____

End of day wrap up: Yes!

Personal goal accomplished?   ☐

Work/School goal accomplished?   ☐

Other accomplishments: _____

_____

_____

Daily Quote

"Focus is the ability to believe in your goal even as your path twists and turns."

~ Linda McLean

What does this mean to me?

_____

_____

_____

_____

_____

_____

_____

_____

_____

_____

_____

Today, I am grateful for...

Date: _____

1. _____

2. _____

3. _____

4. _____

5. _____

6. _____

7. _____

8. _____

9. _____

10. _____

Goals for today:

Personal: _____

Work/School: _____

End of day wrap up: Yes!

Personal goal accomplished?   ☐

Work/School goal accomplished?   ☐

Other accomplishments: _____

_____

_____

Daily Quote

"Seek to discover and learn all that is available to you. Don't waste your time sitting on the fence — jump off and discover the wonderful world you see!"

~ Linda McLean

What does this mean to me?

_____

_____

_____

_____

_____

_____

_____

_____

_____

Today, I am grateful for...

Date: ....

1. ....

2. ....

3. ....

4. ....

5. ....

6. ....

7. ....

8. ....

9. ....

10. ....

Goals for today:

Personal: ....

Work/School: ....

End of day wrap up: Yes!

Personal goal accomplished?   ☐

Work/School goal accomplished?   ☐

Other accomplishments: ....

....

....

Daily Quote

"Learn to forgive yourself first and you'll be stronger for everyone around you...including yourself."

~ Linda McLean

what does this mean to me?

_____

_____

_____

_____

_____

_____

_____

_____

_____

_____

_____

_____

_____

Today, I am grateful for...

Date: _____

1. _____

2. _____

3. _____

4. _____

5. _____

6. _____

7. _____

8. _____

9. _____

10. _____

Goals for today:

Personal: _____

Work/School: _____

End of day wrap up: Yes!

Personal goal accomplished?   ☐

Work/School goal accomplished?   ☐

Other accomplishments: _____

_____

_____

Daily Quote

"A grateful heart has the ability to embrace everything from a different perspective. You will have the power to turn a cloudy day to one filled with rays of sunshine by simply being grateful for the small daily miracles."

~ Linda McLean

What does this mean to me?

_____

_____

_____

_____

_____

_____

_____

_____

_____

_____

Today, I am grateful for...

Date: _____

1. _____

2. _____

3. _____

4. _____

5. _____

6. _____

7. _____

8. _____

9. _____

10. _____

Goals for today:

Personal: _____

Work/School: _____

End of day wrap up: *Yes!*

Personal goal accomplished? ☐

Work/School goal accomplished? ☐

Other accomplishments: _____

_____

_____

Daily Quote

*"Trust that you can achieve what you set out to accomplish.
If an idea was given to you, it is possible for you to achieve it.
Trust your own abilities!"*

~ Linda McLean

What does this mean to me?

Today, I am grateful for...

Date:

1.

2.

3.

4.

5.

6.

7.

8.

9.

10.

Goals for today:

Personal:

Work/School:

End of day wrap up: Yes!

Personal goal accomplished?   ☐

Work/School goal accomplished?   ☐

Other accomplishments:

Daily Quote

"Faith doesn't come by seeing.
Faith comes by believing & feeling."

~ Linda McLean

What does this mean to me?

Today, I am grateful for...

Date: _____

1. _____

2. _____

3. _____

4. _____

5. _____

6. _____

7. _____

8. _____

9. _____

10. _____

Goals for today:

Personal: _____

Work/School: _____

End of day wrap up: Yes!

Personal goal accomplished?   ☐

Work/School goal accomplished?   ☐

Other accomplishments: _____

_____

_____

Daily Quote

*"True happiness relates more to mind and heart.
Happiness that depends mainly on physical or material is not
long lasting; one day it's there, the next day it may not be."*

~ Linda McLean

What does this mean to me?

_____

_____

_____

_____

_____

_____

_____

_____

_____

_____

Today, I am grateful for...

Date: _____

1. _____

2. _____

3. _____

4. _____

5. _____

6. _____

7. _____

8. _____

9. _____

10. _____

Goals for today:

Personal: _____

Work/School: _____

End of day wrap up: Yes!

Personal goal accomplished?   ☐

Work/School goal accomplished?   ☐

Other accomplishments: _____

_____

_____

Daily Quote

"Stop magnifying your problems, change worry time into planning time."

~ Linda McLean

What does this mean to me?

_____

_____

_____

_____

_____

_____

_____

_____

_____

_____

_____

_____

_____

Today, I am grateful for...

Date: ....

1. ....

2. ....

3. ....

4. ....

5. ....

6. ....

7. ....

8. ....

9. ....

10. ....

Goals for today:

Personal: ....

Work/School: ....

End of day wrap up: Yes!

Personal goal accomplished?   ☐

Work/School goal accomplished?   ☐

Other accomplishments: ....

....

....

Daily Quote

"Seek positive, winning role models and learn to apply the lessons you learn from them."

~ Linda McLean

What does this mean to me?

_____

_____

_____

_____

_____

_____

_____

_____

_____

_____

_____

_____

_____

Today, I am grateful for...

Date: _____

1. _____

2. _____

3. _____

4. _____

5. _____

6. _____

7. _____

8. _____

9. _____

10. _____

Goals for today:

Personal: _____

Work/School: _____

End of day wrap up:　　　　Yes!

Personal goal accomplished?　　☐

Work/School goal accomplished?　☐

Other accomplishments: _____

_____

_____

Daily Quote

"Smiling is one tool that when used,
brings joy to you and all others around you.
Carry it with you every day and use it!"

~ Linda McLean

What does this mean to me?

Today, I am grateful for...

Date: _____

1. _____
2. _____
3. _____
4. _____
5. _____
6. _____
7. _____
8. _____
9. _____
10. _____

Goals for today:

Personal: _____

Work/School: _____

End of day wrap up: Yes!

Personal goal accomplished?   ☐

Work/School goal accomplished?   ☐

Other accomplishments: _____

_____

_____

Congratulations!

Congratulations on your commitment in recognizing what you are grateful for on a daily basis. May you continue on your journey of gratitude and awareness. As you do, you will reach new levels in your life.

We strongly recommend you continue with this personal development process. By doing so, you'll reach incredible levels of success and happiness.

Yours for greater success,

Follow Linda on:

 *www.facebook.com/Linda.McLean.Consultant.Author.Speaker*

 *@LindaMMcLean*

www.linkedin.com/in/mcleaninternational

For a new Gratitude Journal or other personal development products, please visit: www.GratitudeJournal.net. Or call: 1-888-572-8326

About the Author

Linda McLean makes it her business to help you catapult your career, business or personal life to the next level. She does this by empowering you to access your inner strengths and desires. Then incorporates proven systems to create your personal roadmap to success and develop your leadership potential.

Linda provides executive, business and life coaching services to corporations, organizations and individuals. As a coach, she works with individuals seeking to increase productivity, bottom line revenue results and personal growth.

As a speaker, Linda motivates and inspires. Her keynotes and presentations are based on strong principles of integrity in leadership, consistent communication and proven business principles.

Linda is a #1 International Bestselling Author, International Speaker, member of the National Speakers Association, accomplished Business and Life coach with over 25 years of experience, and CEO/founder of McLean International LLC.

If you are interested in having Linda McLean present to your organization or wish to receive more information about her presentations, coaching programs or personal development products, call toll free: 1-888-572-8326 or visit: www.McleanInternational.com.

CPSIA information can be obtained at www.ICGtesting.com
Printed in the USA
BVOW032353300513

322065BV00002B/10/P